Clinical Dharma

A Path for Healers and Helpers

Stephen Dansiger, PsyD, MFT

Printed in the United States of America

First Printing, 2016

ISBN-13:   978-0692756522
ISBN-10:   0692756523

Publisher: StartAgain Media
Book Design: Averi Endow
Editor: Shannon Flynn
Author Photo: Gen Max

For all inquiries regarding Clinical Dharma and StartAgain Media
go to:
www.drdansiger.com

For all my teachers, students, colleagues and clients... past, present and future

And for my two greatest teachers, Sadie and Sabrina

Contents

FOREWORD

Dr. Stephen Dansiger is one of the many people who have lived a parallel path to my own. In my youth, I was a West Coast punk rock drug addict that eventually turned to recovery, Dharma and clinical training, while Stephen lived the East Coast version of the Dharma Punx path. He and I connected through mutual friends many years ago and it was one of those moments of recognition, another brother on the path, a survivor of the 80s punk scene, a fellow recovering addict, a Dharma practitioner and clinical colleague. Dr. Dansiger is the real deal. He practices what he teaches, he teaches what he knows from direct experience and application.

In this clear and accessible book on the integration of clinical practice and Dharma practice he offers us deep and transformative teachings and stories that illuminate the Buddhist path in such a way that both the long term practitioner and the newly initiated of both or either paths will be served.

The Four Noble Truths of the Buddha fit perfectly with the path of service and healing that we undertake as clinicians and teachers. All of the Buddhas' teachings have the goal of helping the individual to end suffering, all clinical practices share this goal. When we turn toward the suffering rather than away from it the healing begins. When we establish mindfulness we see how we are creating the unnecessary level of suffering on top of our already difficult experiences. We see suffering and the causes of suffering. Then we can open to the healing we all seek, the healing that comes from compassion for pain, non-clinging to pleasure and not taking it all so personal. This is just what it's like to have a mind and body, to be human.

The more we understand ourselves and how we have created our own suffering, the better equipped we will be to help guide our clients or patients in their attempts to understand and heal. As Dr. Dansiger points out, the Buddhas' teachings are laid out as a treatment plan, an ancient medical model that diagnoses and cures the causes of suffering. This book will prove to be a very important resource for all of us in the helping professions.

May all good things come of your life's energy,

Noah Levine
Refuge Recovery – Los Angeles - 2016

PREFACE

I humbly present this small book to you. It was born from my love of the Dharma, my love of the helping and healing professions, and my sincere feeling of compassion for all those on both sides of the helping dyad. For many years I have had the opportunity to practice in a variety of realms. In the world of education, I saw teachers stretched thin on internal and external resources. In social justice work, I saw deep convictions forged into concrete actions, sometimes leaving the actor without any space for self-care. In the healing professions currently, I feel myself leaning into compassion for my colleagues as heartily as for our charges.

I admit it. My view became quite skewed due to my introduction to the Dharma over 25 years ago. My Buddhist mindfulness practice has anchored and guided my actions ever since I started sitting. Over this time I have watched mindfulness go on the cover of magazines, even having entire magazines devoted to it. I have seen it enter into the world of modern psychology, and seen the scientific research back up its merits.

I wrote Clinical Dharma to point us back to the original formulation of the historical Buddha in order to find a sustainable path for the healer and helper. Those of us who choose to help, or are karmically placed in that position through circumstances, need to find ways to alleviate our own suffering in order to truly be able to provide that care for others. I wrote this book in some ways to help myself, and I hope it can provide a snowball effect. We need each other, I think. We need each other in order to help each other.

I have many people to thank. Some were instrumental in building me into the healer and helper I am today, some who literally helped me to write and create the book. There are some who I am sure I will forget to mention by name, and my apologies for that up front. Thank you to Noah Levine for his support in the Dharma and with Refuge Recovery Centers. Thanks to Dr. Josh Lichtman for being my first reader. Thanks to the clinicians and Dharma teachers at Refuge Recovery and everyone on the staff. Thanks to the entire Against the Stream sangha for their practice. Thank you to Averi Endow for her tireless work on behalf of StartAgain Media and all of her beautiful images and designs. Thank you to Shannon Flynn for her nuanced editing of the manuscript. Thank you to Melanie Vesey for her support, especially during the writing process. A big thank you to Johnny Fisher for helping me move forward with all of my work in 2016. Thank you to Michael Kink and to all my friends back in NYC, you all know who you are, you are my strength, my loving kindness factory, the place and the people that taught me how to do any of this. Thank you to Dr. Jamie Marich for your friendship, for your own writing, the opportunity to be part of the

Institute for Creative Mindfulness, the opportunity to be your colleague and writing partner. Thank you to Andrew Leeds and everyone else who has either trained me, supervised me, or encouraged me to become the therapist I am today. Thank you to everyone from my Zen community in NYC, especially Seigan Ed Glassing. Thank you to Jim Tynan, Randy Burns, the late Saul Lambert and Peter Gallway for helping me without asking for any return. Thank you so much to the late Simon Eckels, who gave me the emotional CPR that allowed me to continue on. Thanks to Dr. Angela Liu. Thanks to all the wonderful ancient and present day Buddhist teachers who have offered their wisdom to us. Thank you to Tanya Odom and every other social justice educator I have been trained by, worked beside or trained. Thank you to Dr. Francine Shapiro for her offering of EMDR Therapy. Thank you to my wife Sabrina and to all of my extended family and ancestors. Thank you to my daughter Sadie Dansiger, who teaches me every day that presence, loving kindness and compassion are always available and appreciated. And lastly, thanks to the Three Jewels... Buddha, Dharma and Sangha.

May this book have some small impact for at least one person on the path leading to liberation.

Stephen Dansiger
Los Angeles, CA

CHAPTER 1

THE TRUTH OF SUFFERING

The Truth of Suffering

There may be many reasons why you have chosen to read this book. You may be simply curious. You may have had it recommended to you by a friend, colleague or a website tracking your interests. It may be that you are fond of one or both of the words in the title. Those of you drawn to "clinical" may have an idea of how this book might help you in those endeavors. Others pulled in by the word "dharma" may have an intimate relationship with the Dharma or may have a loose idea of its definition, positing it to be some kind of esoteric set of beliefs.

Regardless of the micro reason you picked up this book or downloaded it on your device, it is only an aspect of the greater reason why we do anything in this world. I have written this book, and you are choosing to read it, because life contains dukkha, or suffering. We have been born into a body and because of this we are destined to die, and herein lies the most basic and inescapable construct of our suffering. The First Noble Truth of the Buddha, this truth of suffering, is why we would pick up such a book as this. And we would pick up this book rather than an episode of the latest tragicomic web series based on our desire to perhaps find a way to alleviate our suffering and the suffering of others, rather than temporarily escape into further delusion.

I have nothing against tragicomic attempts to escape through applied delusion; I have engaged in much of that myself. I can even point to it as a healing force at times, and maybe even a source of great insight. There has been cultivated in me, however, through a number of causes and conditions, a sincere desire to practice the Buddha Dharma and through that practice to bring about the end of suffering. The Four Noble Truths and the Eightfold Path point in that direction, and in that direction I choose to walk, sometimes haltingly, sometimes at a sprint. At either speed, my motivator is the weight and depth of the First Noble Truth. When first encountered it may be experienced as a bummer and an invitation to move far away from the Buddhist path. Upon deeper inspection, its truth becomes so simple and clear that I have thought at times that I might be moved to reply to the Buddha if he were to appear before me, "Hey, that first truth... um... yeah... duh." The reality of suffering is always so close at hand, multiple times a day, sometimes with nuance, sometimes with all the subtlety of a hammer blow to the head. If there were only one Noble Truth, we would be in big trouble. But this truth of suffering is more than anything the reality check we need to engage in so that we may then walk the path through it, and beyond it, to the other shore.

So the Dharma as espoused by the Buddha, resting on the foundation of suffering, seems like a perfectly designed template for healing. As opposed to us all being sinners, we are all sick and suffering. The word clinical defines another pathway for those who wish to alleviate suffering. Those who have picked up this book who were drawn to the word clinical may be someone in any of the helping professions. There may be medical doctors who seek to find new ways to do no harm. There may be nurses who seek answers for their own suffering that comes from the constant interaction with suffering of others on a physical level. Psychologists who work with traumatized clients may need a new pair of glasses through which to view these experiences. Family therapists may need to feel that the deep suffering of dysfunctional families can have some meaning and some resolution. It may be also the person Jacquelyn Small describes in the her book Becoming Naturally Therapeutic (1989): the friend or family member who does not become a professional healer, but rather chooses to hone these skills for the benefit of the people around them. It can be the yoga teacher, the massage therapist, the Employment Assistance Program (EAP) director, or the mindfulness meditation instructor. I have written this book for all of you because I know you suffer, I know you are drawn to your clinical paths because of suffering, and I know the Dharma to be a holistic and practical healing answer to the infinitely deep question of suffering.

There is no hierarchy of suffering in this construct. Suffering is most evident in sickness, old age and death. These are some of the grosser aspects of suffering that bring us to our professions. In that spirit, a client told me today they were absolutely through with just surviving. They believe in their heart of hearts that they have a life to live. So we who are helpers utilize our gifts, our skills and our craft in order to bring an end to the gerbil wheel of survival. We facilitate in so many different ways the process of long-suffering individuals stepping off the treadmill, feeling their feet on solid ground and touching the earth, sometimes for the first time. From that grounded place, anything is possible. It is never simple or easy, but it is forever possible.

So how do we as healers interpret the first truth? How do we work with it? How do we use it as a springboard to our own practice? It is said that the reason why wisdom is the first factor of the Eight Fold Path is that we need just enough wisdom to know that beginning this practice and this path would be a good idea. Much wisdom is further garnered through the practice, but we will not even consider it if stuck in the delusion that there is no point to seeking a different way of seeing, a different way of experiencing reality.

So our interpretation of the first truth can be something like this -- I have seen suffering in its many forms, in myself and others, and I am utterly moved to find some way that I can end that suffering, or at least reduce it. This first truth is complete. It states something so simple and in the end so obvious that one could easily walk past it and not engage with it, but rather just fall into its spell. All around us are people lost in greed, hatred and delusion, so much in delusion that they are unaware of their confusion. All around us are people desperately trying to win a fist fight with impermanence, who are caught in the web of their suffering and the suffering of others, and equally as desperately, are trying to find solace in the creation and the satisfaction of all things I, me, and mine.

As someone moved to be there for others, a simple yet elegant way to maintain our direction and our purpose while also keeping our sanity is for us to gain a deeper insight into the truth of suffering. Our springboard may have been a direct experience of our own suffering or the suffering of a loved one, or maybe even the suffering of a distant other. Regardless, our successful maintenance of a life as a helper depends on our going beyond our initial starting point and investigating suffering with a spirit of curiosity.

As I write this, I have recently been in a phase of seeing my own suffering in the form of wanting to do more than I possibly have time for, and falling toward overextending myself. This is very different than the beginning of my path to becoming a healer, born of the deep, greedy, angry and confused suffering of addiction, which was complicated by depression and anxiety that had lives of their own. When I got sober in a twelve step program, I was introduced to the concept that my suffering could be uniquely useful to another sufferer, and that through helping someone else there would be a number of internal and external benefits, including continuing to stay sober myself. From there I have followed the bouncing ball of suffering in many directions -- sitting meditation with others; trying to ease the suffering of ignorance by becoming a high school teacher; becoming an educator in the world of diversity, conflict resolution and anger management; becoming a therapist and a therapist educator; and becoming a husband and father. Throughout this journey, my relationship with the First Truth has changed constantly, while the truth itself has remained the same.

How strange that something so intrinsically sad could anchor me to the even greater truth of the possibility of the end of suffering. It is difficult to accept perhaps, but once accepted, life becomes available for living in the moment. The truth of the intensely joyful energy of helping others, of honoring our interconnectedness through loving care, becomes manifest from this place. I see this truth in action every day, and I am incredibly grateful for it. My hope is that this gratitude and joy might be contagious. The life of the helper can be one of engagement, connectedness, healing and joy in the presence of suffering.

Moving on to the Second Truth, an analysis of the causes of suffering can help deepen our insight and provide more energy toward our goal of healing ourselves and others. Before I can help effectively, I need to know causes and conditions.

CHAPTER 2

THE CAUSE OF SUFFERING IS
CRAVING, AVERSION, AND
ATTACHMENT

The Cause of Suffering is Craving, Aversion and Attachment

Life is not suffering in a vacuum. Suffering has a cause. Identification of that cause can lead to healing. This is what Buddha declared 2600 years ago, and this is what healers of all kinds have asserted for millennia. Ignorance of causes and conditions allows wounds to fester, and allows for ongoing confusion and pain. Buddha saw that the root cause of our suffering was the pursuit of pleasure and the fleeing from pain, and attachment to the states of being that come from this dance of pursuit and flight. My sanity and my serenity are directly related to the degree to which I can accept and work with my current conditions. If I crave conditions other than those that I encounter, or desire to get away from those sensations and situations that I find disagreeable, suffering commences. If I become attached to a pleasurable state and it goes away, I suffer.

This aversion to pain and attraction to pleasure is not a dance between good and evil. Contained within are the roots of survival. I am on the lookout for that which would harm me so that I can avoid it and live on, and am simultaneously seeking those pleasant or harmless events and beings so that I might further thrive. These instincts are what have driven evolution for millions of years. What evolution also brought us was the human experience, the development of the neocortex and the development of a more complex, more layered existence. With our expanded consciousness, we live with a double-edged sword. I am more artist than scientist, but what I have been led to discover by the scientists in my field is this -- the properly trained mind, with all three brains (reptilian, limbic and neocortical) working in consort, each supporting and informing the other, will adaptively process information and memories and allow us to transcend simple animal survival reactions while remaining grounded in direct experience. On the creative and spiritual side, this is what I believe the proverbial "They" are referring to when they speak of mind, body and spirit.

How does this binary of pleasure and pain impact the healer? In some ways the fulcrum upon which the entire dilemma rests is that of the healer's attraction toward and attachment to seeking the pleasure of providing the cure. Books upon books, and twelve-step meetings and other support groups across the world are dedicated to the difficulties faced by the codependent, the helper who becomes an accidental enabler of the person with whom they have a caring relationship. The life of the healer is a codependent nightmare waiting to happen. For many years, the mantra around this issue I was given was to be a "caregiver, not a caretaker." How do I be there for a suffering being without being dragged into my own suffering of attaching to the result?

In Catskills joke form: "What's the difference between God and a doctor? God doesn't think he's a doctor." This does not have to be limited to the medical profession, nor does it have to be a put down. It is a warning to the healer in a one liner. The most likely place for suffering to be generated for healers or helpers is at this crossroads of whether or not they will be able to let go of the result. As the helper, if I allow myself to attach to the result, believing that some version of "I" has accomplished a great healing task and bask in the pleasure of that, I have created suffering for myself. If I allow myself to get lost in the pain of the other, if I get into the mud with them in the name of a false compassion (false not because of nefarious intent, but born of delusion), then I have created suffering for myself, and perhaps even multiplied the suffering of the other. The cause of suffering for the helper is the craving for a positive result or an aversion to a negative result and an attachment to the result, regardless.

I am not writing these words from up on high, in an ivory tower or otherwise. I have lived through this moment-to-moment quandary at different levels of consciousness for more than twenty-five years, as a sponsor to people in recovery, as an educator and as a therapist. I did not catapult into some state of Nirvana at any juncture, never to make the same mistakes again. Time after time, especially in the beginning of each of those careers, the first one avocational, and then as a professional, I found myself faced not only with the suffering of the other but with my own pain. How difficult it is to detach with love, to respect the process of the other and to be helpful without being invasive! How difficult it is to not make this helping all about myself! How difficult it is to fail. How difficult it is to cut through the delusion of success versus failure.

How is success versus failure delusion? In its very root of striving. And in its essence of attachment to a result. Only in attachment to a result can there be success or failure. This does not mean we do not have goals in our helping schema. The surgeon hopes to clear away the sickness in the body. The therapist sets the intention of providing emotional healing for the client. The yoga teacher holds the space, teaches poses and creates sets with a body of knowledge behind them that points toward a hoped-for result. The caregiver wipes the sweat off the brow of the patient and changes their linens, hoping they become more comfortable. The key to this question is when are we striving unhealthily toward suffering and when are we setting intention to provide care, while letting go of the end result?

One reason why there is so much suffering in this world is that this question cannot be answered perfectly, permanently and scientifically, once and for all. This human experience is an ongoing experiment; that word experiment rings true because of the truth of impermanence. The Buddha taught that there are three marks of existence, with dukkha or suffering placed second on the list. Some of that suffering is caused by our resistance to the first characteristic, that of impermanence. More dukkha manifests from our fighting the third characteristic, that of the lack of a permanent or solid "I" to land on. Suffering increases when I mistake the impermanent moment-to-moment change of all mind and matter to be solid and permanent. Suffering increases when I attach to results, taking things personally, riding the intense tsunami waves of the thrill of accomplishment and the despair of the absolute truth of old age, sickness and death, all collapsing into and onto an imagined solid self.

This does not mean we are not to feel our feelings. In fact, it is clear that if we do not feel our feelings, we will suffer in even greater measure as we are blindsided by those stuffed emotions at some later date, in some other form. Rather, we are encouraged by the Buddha, and the women and men who have taught after his time, to embrace the truth of impermanence, dukkha and not-self. Buddha instructed that of all the insights that might bring about an end to suffering, deep insight into impermanence could be the portal to a good rebirth. Seen in a worldly, in-the-moment context, this can be referencing the many rebirths we experience every day, each moment passing into the next equally impermanent moment.

I have often shared that at a certain point in my recovery, I was able to feel my feelings in chronological order. Instead of those feelings building and creating a mistaken sense of identity, I am able to feel them and also watch them change, move, transform, disappear. Here is where the craving can end, thereby relieving the healer of the extra suffering unique to the helping process. Here it's possible to end the craving for a permanent solution to impermanence: the attachment to my being able to cure the other in perpetuity to my own specifications and designs. This can come to pass through deep insight into the nature of this craving for permanence, this aversion to old age, sickness and death, this attachment to outcomes. The truth of impermanence and of my own limitations within that reality can help set the helper free.

The first Noble Truth of the Buddha was our diagnosis. This Second Truth is the identification of the causes. Now having gained insight into the causes, we can move on to seeing if there might be a cure.

CHAPTER 3

SUFFERING CAN END

Suffering Can End

Sometimes our entry into the field of helping is built on desperation. There may not be an intrinsic belief that suffering can end. Often these are the roots of codependence being sown. The compassion that starts the process is by no means pathological, but the resulting snowball effect of the toxins of enabling, soul sucking, denial, head banging, burnout and resentment can take their toll and become the norm. This is an extreme description of the unfortunate outcome of helping that is not tethered to the reciprocal nature of service or the interconnectedness of being. It is not meant as a Scared Straight tactic. It is, however, meant to stop us all in our tracks as we move into the Third Truth of the Buddha as it pertains to our role as helpers.

There can be end to suffering, proclaimed the Buddha as his Third Noble Truth. There are only Four Noble Truths, and this is one of them. That should be enough to wake us up. But this truth is so radical, so definitive, that it is only natural that we might either dig our feet in deeply and become ready to fight this truth or at least debate it, or we might disappear into a haze of denial and delusion. Either way, we only have these reactions because we are human beings. As human beings, as beings, we have a survival instinct, and this survival instinct makes us wary of our surroundings as a first response to stimuli. This more complex stimulus of the Third Truth is no different than other learning dilemmas we have had throughout our lives. Having had the experience so deeply of the first two truths, that of suffering and the causes of suffering, it might be hard to believe at any level that this profound suffering and these foundational cravings and attachments can abate, let alone end. I have to say for myself, each time I wake up in the morning, it is another call to action for my own wrestling match with the Third Truth.

Both personally and professionally, my relationship with diagnosable addiction problems has been my successful entry point into the Third Truth. Using the World Health Organization definition of addiction, I am able to connect with the larger frame of craving and attachment through its cinematic close-up: Addiction is the "compulsive, repetitive use of a substance (or a behavior) despite negative consequences." The compulsion and repetition define the contours of craving, aversion and attachment like a blind person traversing through the woods of life. The image I often use for myself is that of "take me to your leader..." In the throes of my addiction, I could not imagine — in fact, I did not bother to imagine -- how to do life without these compulsions in repetition. The key to the definition, however, is "despite negative consequences." Despite the karmic fruits of my actions that are fed or altered by the compulsive and repetitive use of the substance, I continue on in the same way. The human condition is such that even without substances, we will generally engage in lower level (and sometimes equal or higher level) consequences of our actions built on our ongoing craving, aversion and attachment. The moral of this particular story, however, is this -- that recovery from diagnosable addiction acts as a proof of the theorem of the Third Truth. If I am able to change my karma in regards to substances and/or behaviors through changing or abstaining from these compulsive and repetitive behaviors, then suffering can end.

A flag I planted long ago in my own recovery and helping history is in the notion that codependence is itself an addiction. I met the criteria fully, as I was compulsively, repetitively focused on the other, despite negative consequences. Seen through that lens, once again I can journey to find recovery from this specific manifestation of suffering, and find that suffering can end. What does this look like in this arena? It is seen through the end of craving for a particular result for the person being helped. It is seen through the end of aversion for the person who finds a solution to their suffering that is outside our own comfort zone or theoretical orientation. It is seen through the ability to apply loving detachment in our helping relationships, maintaining our compassionate touch while providing boundaries that respect both self and other. When I engage in boundary crossing, unhealthy attachment, and a closed and fixed view of the nature of healing, that is the codependency addiction at play. This manifestation of suffering can end.

So if suffering can end, and that end can come through the ending of craving, aversion and attachment, how can we facilitate this in ourselves and others? That answer is more fully developed in the Fourth Noble Truth, but some of it can be addressed here as part of the Third. Craving can be addressed through renunciation and restraint. Renunciation is a strong word that has the whiff of religiosity and of monasticism. Indeed, renunciation to its fullest extent can mean the shaving of the head, the wearing of simple robes, acquiring food by begging with a bowl, and doing without money or sexual relationships. Maybe think of these things as Extreme Sports Renunciation. In our 21st century world where lay people in ever increasing numbers are seeking spiritual practice, and in particular those dedicated to Buddhist practice, what does renunciation look like?

Actually, it looks much like it did 2600 years ago for those who did not live the life of the monastic. A willingness to practice simple restraint when it comes to the five senses is a wonderful way to start. Being able to have a mindful relationship with my food intake, my sense of touch, what I take in with my eyes and ears, all of this helps me to develop the spirit of the renunciate. We do not need to get rid of everything, all our belongings and experiences, but rather develop a mindful relationship with them that allows us to more deeply experience each moment with our senses and our consciousness.

One of my greatest (ongoing) lessons in renunciation is when some pain or itch develops in or on my body while I am sitting. Having trained in a Zen monastery for many years, there was an emphasis on posture and on holding completely still. My very normal human response to pain or even just slight discomfort is to move a little bit in my seat, maybe move my leg a couple of inches to the left, or perhaps lift my hand toward my face and blissfully scratch the itch on my cheek. Sometimes I do this mindlessly, other times with full forethought (a few seconds worth) and intentional volition. Over the years as I have increasingly renounced those reactions to these urges, I have noticed subtle changes in my ability to filter the spirit of renunciation into my day-to-day life.

It may sound ridiculous to those newer to practice, or even to those trained in traditions where posture and stillness may not have been as focused upon, but think about it for a moment. We are coming from the perspective that all of this relates to dukkha -- that my unscratched itch, although a far lesser form of suffering than a career disappointment, or the end of a relationship, or a debilitating illness, is suffering nonetheless. Staying perfectly still and breathing quietly in order not to disturb others, simply noticing and tracking the little aches and pains and other aversions and cravings as they come and go -- this is the practice. And what these tiny acts of renunciation accomplish is much like many reps with weights in the gym. Strength is built, endurance is established, and patience becomes a central characteristic. Patience and endurance become equanimity; strength becomes compassion. We develop a spirit of friendliness toward our bodies, toward our pains and our itches, a spirit of loving kindness.

Lastly, one of the greatest lessons about the difference between pain and suffering has also been revealed to me through these simple acts of renunciation. When I do go ahead and move my leg a little bit to attempt to get relief, my unscientific anecdotal estimate is that about 90 percent of the time I end up in more pain than before I moved my leg. So by renouncing the movement of the aching limb, I actually decrease suffering in the long term. Trying to change my reality fails, much like my attempts through drugs, alcohol and various other substances and behaviors. Who knew that saying no to the craving for a fingernail across an itchy nose would in the long run build equanimity, even in the face of the most difficult circumstances? I know that I didn't know that. I just kept practicing diligently and found out for myself, which is what the Buddha promised -- that I could have the experience he had.

So suffering can end. It can end by renouncing its causes of craving, aversion and clinging. The Fourth Noble Truth is the prescription, an apt way to put it for helpers. And what better prescriber is there than the talented and insightful psychologist, Siddhartha Gautama?

CHAPTER 4

THE EIGHT FOLD PATH
PRESCRIPTION

The 8 Fold Path Prescription

Having come to the belief that suffering can end, then there must be a formula or at least some guidelines for the path. When at first the Buddha was enlightened, he was reticent about trying to share the experience with anyone, as he felt that no one would understand. He said to a disciple who asked about it that people had "too much dust in their eyes" to receive this Dharma. The response to Buddha was that he should teach to those who maybe had even just a little less dust in their eyes. Buddha used the model of medicine at the time, Ayurveda, to try to explain the ways in which one could cultivate the same experience he had experienced. We have already spoken about the diagnosis, the symptoms, and the proposed cure. The Fourth Truth is the prescription, the medicine. The medicine is a path, a practical guide to living, grounded in wisdom, compassionately ethical behavior, and meditation.

The first factor in the Eight Fold Path is wisdom, or right understanding. Is this some kind of intellectual exercise of fact gathering, memorization and taking a test? Is it simply the wisdom of day-to-day experience, accumulated over the years of a life span? It would seem it might be more complex than all that. The initial wisdom is the intuitive knowledge that acquiring this wisdom and acting upon it might bring a positive outcome. The rest of the initial understanding is grounded in the three marks of existence. The minute I am able to grasp impermanence, even ever so slightly, I can begin to see some of the folly of my craving and clinging. The moment I touch upon suffering, whether my own or that of another, I can see, touch and feel the momentous goal that the end of suffering represents. And when I experience even somewhat the pain of reveling in, rolling around in, celebrating endlessly and focusing like a laser beam on the seemingly constant I/Me/Mine, I start to sense the unskillfulness of that proposition. These three insights, even at their beginning stages, and seemingly only superficially and intellectually digested, are the basis of right understanding.

Then there is right intention. The setting of intention may seem like a to-do list or a variation on New Year's resolutions. One might even envision a one-year, five-year or ten-year plan. With just a little bit of right understanding of the Three Marks, intention becomes much broader and yet more concentrated at the same time. In a world marked by impermanence, intention must be set again and again, not just day to day, but moment to moment. In a world marked by suffering, the intention must be deeply rooted in the foundational motivation to end suffering. And in a world marked by not-self, intention must come from a different, deeper, more profound sense of a selfless self in order to end suffering. When the self is neutralized in this way, there is no one to do the clinging, and no one to take offense and feel aversion. Again, this is not Night of the Living

Dead, a permanent zombie movie or a phone off the hook with a dial tone. It is not an esoteric metaphysical statement of a lack of a being, of a lack of personality or of an inherent inability to continue to relate to others and to the world. It is a very practical reimagining of the ego, of he or she who is living in the world, acting and speaking in the world. It is a framework based on a direct experience that the Buddha had after almost thirty years of life as a sheltered royal, seven years of living as a renunciate, and seven days under the Bodhi tree. He saw directly into impermanence; he saw directly into suffering; he saw directly through his small "s" self, the construct of his ego. And once he saw that he could perhaps help those with less dust in their eyes, he set the intention to teach, and he did that for forty-five years.

In the words of many in recovery, "He did it so we don't have to." We don't have to live as monastics; we don't have to teach ceaselessly for forty-five years. In fact, in one sutra, Buddha starts by saying that years of practice will bring the practitioner to these direct experiences, and by the end of the sutra he has winnowed it down to a seven-day requirement. My experience has borne this out through many retreats, but also through days of dedicated practice while firmly entrenched in my lay life, including my life of helping others. The turnkey event is my setting of intention, the intention of paying attention to the rest of the path laid out in front of me.

The Ethical Factors are incredibly important to the Eight Fold Path, and particularly so in this framework of Clinical Dharma. Right Speech can be looked at as knowing that our words have power, power over ourselves and power over the other. Our words have the infinite power to heal and unfortunately the great power to do harm. Speech leads the procession of ethical factors because in the human experience, language most often leads thought and action. There is the self-talk that can be brutal for ourselves and for those we help, and there is the outward communication that can change the landscape in a syllable. When I was running a Juvenile Diversion program for young people convicted of hate crimes in New York City, I would co-facilitate most of the workshops. I worked regularly with a Holocaust survivor who would inevitably bring tears to the hardest of the hard. His main point when he told his story was this: "The Holocaust did not start with broken glass and gas chambers, it started with words." Words leading to genocide is the worst case scenario; words leading to enlightenment is the best case scenario. In between are endless opportunities to practice creating no harm or less harm with our speech.

Right Action essentially defines all of the rest that we do beyond words. In a state of mindfulness, the nature of action and the mental and emotional act of self reflection become more intertwined. Over time, actions and speech that have been heavily considered prior to their launching take on a very different character from impulsive acts of craving, clinging and aversion. As an educator, and later as a therapist, I would often counsel my students and clients in the art of allowing for a first thought and a second thought, and even a third thought to arise before forming any words or taking any actions. And then, a hindsight approach to action can actually be effective, as I reflect on the previous day's actions as lessons rather than wet noodles with which to beat myself.

The last ethical factor is of course important to the Eight Fold Path in general, but it is critical when thinking of Clinical Dharma. Right Livelihood -- its definition, its practice, its intricacies -- is the real inspiration for writing this book. When I was living at the monastery, there was a guest Zen Master who visited from Japan. I was very early in my monastic practice and was coming off a very difficult stretch in my lay life. I did not feel particularly strong in my practice or in my day to day. When this visiting teacher asked me what my practice was, I did not have a pithy Zen answer prepared (or unprepared, as it should be). I did however say, as spontaneously as I was capable of at that moment, "right livelihood." It was the only practice that I felt I had been engaged in over the last year or so, as my impression was that the wheels had come off everything else. To my surprise, and at that moment, shame, the teacher laughed and looked at me quizzically.

This laugh and the RCA Victor dog look that he gave me are part of what drives the writing of this book, and the creation of the workshops and retreats that go with it. For many in the helping professions, Right Livelihood is what provides the first portal into practice, into dharma, whether or not the person is studying Buddha Dharma. And my experience has been that one can begin to cultivate a Dharma practice through any of the 8 factors, the 4 truths, the 3 marks, even the 5 hindrances of sensual desire, ill will, sloth/torpor, restlessness/worry and doubt. If you are a professional or non-professional helper who has been drawn to this book and have never meditated in your life, or have only touched upon mindfulness lightly or briefly, then that is Right Livelihood acting as the entry way to practice.

The last three factors all have to do with meditation. Right Effort means that I am going to put the correct energy and practice into my mindfulness and concentration at any given time. Right Mindfulness is the cultivation of non-judgmental awareness, infused with acceptance of "what is." All the elements of the Dharma contribute to this acceptance, with meditation being the anchor and central vortex for collecting that energy and insight. Right Concentration helps us to deepen our state of mindfulness and to retrain the brain out of its monkey mind ways, ceasing the swinging from branch to branch for even a moment, thus showing our minds a different type of activity and a new perspective.

This is the path laid out by the Buddha, designed to provide a very practical guide to living mindfully and skillfully. For the helper, being mindful of our inner experience as well as our relational presence in a helping or healing posture with someone gives us a greater chance to connect, not only for the benefit of the two in this engagement, but for all beings. The more we learn about and experience lessons in the power of skillful action as healers and helpers, the more the web of mindfulness, loving kindness, compassion and equanimity spreads. As we break down the Eight Fold Path in the following chapters, see where your own experience matches that of these words. Also see where your experience deviates or is challenged by these words. My encouragement to all of us is to have our own direct experience, taking on what resonates and discarding that which does not fit. The Eight Fold Path is simply a winding road that helps us to navigate our own direct experiences mindfully, hopefully more skillfully, and as Jack Kornfield put it, as A Path with Heart. Our heart can open and grow, within ourselves and in relation to the other.

CHAPTER 5

RIGHT UNDERSTANDING

Right Understanding

Now that the path of the Buddha has been laid out, we can consider the eight aspects of that path. It is presented as a list in a specific order mostly because that is how we can read them and digest them. That does not mean we have to follow them as if marching, one after the other, marking our successes and moving on. However, wisdom or right understanding leads the procession because it holds great power and importance. There are those who would put wisdom at the end, for is it not wisdom that we grow into through the process of the path? Perhaps, but the path will be more clearly seen through the prism of the essence of the specific wisdom that is received and then applied. This wisdom is different in some ways than that understanding we might traditionally think of in the Western psychological community. And looking through that Buddhist prism shows us that the wisdom found at the end is not so much an end as a beginning of another loop or pass at the path.

What is this right understanding that is necessary to begin our path? And what of it can be seen as unique or even essential in Clinical Dharma? What I have read time and again and have been told directly in equal measure is that I must have at least enough wisdom and understanding to believe that it would be wise to continue with the other seven factors of the path. This wisdom can be revealed in many different ways. Some come to this wisdom from a singular experience or event, while most come to it in the way described by William James and coopted by Bill Wilson for AA, which is the spiritual experience of the "educational variety." That education is an unfolding, progression and evolution of wisdom over time. One of my teachers spoke of "mini-enlightenments." Other teachers have pointed out the wisdom of transformation in favor of the wisdom of sudden, overwhelming and complete enlightenment found in other quarters. My feeling is that nobody is wrong here, they are only pointing to different aspects of a greater truth that is revealed a little bit differently to different people. Sometimes a combination of educational and sudden becomes one's experience.

My own path has been strewn with a variety of transformative events, experiences and people. In hindsight, I am able to see slow progressions. I am also able to see times where I was rocked to the core, and nothing was the same again. These two types of enlightenment or wisdom gathering are not in competition, nor is one better than the other. The key to the power of all of the transformations is that they are directly experienced. Buddha taught about the innate wisdom that we all have, and how to access this wisdom. When first faced with teaching it, he balked because what he had directly experienced was beyond words, so much so that he was convinced that absolutely no one would understand it. As he began teaching, however, many of his disciples had their own immediate and overwhelming direct experience of the truth. So contrary to his original fear, when presented from a place of infinitely wise understanding, he found that rapid transformation is possible.

I can point back to a few times in my life that changed the game in a moment or in a night. There were the last three beers that I drank. I was long into my attempts to manage and control my drinking, followed by an attempt to remain abstinent with no real assistance. I went out with friends to hear some music at the original Knitting Factory, and then we went for drinks. I was trying to not drink that night. I was sitting between my current girlfriend and my ex-girlfriend. My current girlfriend was my one person who was working on the no-drinking project with me. At some point in the evening, my ex said that I was very boring when I didn't drink. I am pretty sure she was just kidding around, but my drinking brain took her very seriously. I ordered a beer, a Rolling Rock, to be specific. The sudden transformation that took place over the next couple of hours was this: The first beer I drank was very soothing. All the edges I wanted to come off came off, and I felt more securely placed in the room. With the second beer, I catapulted directly into lampshade mode, and became (a little too much) the life of the party. Finally, I had a third beer and very quickly became the morose, even suicidal drunk I had become. My fourteen-year drinking history and attendant behaviors had been compressed into three

Rolling Rocks. Before the night was through, I was very clear that this was not sustainable; in fact, it was a whole lot of suffering. I didn't have the language for it at the time, but my accumulated wisdom about my drinking was signed and sealed by this particular direct experience of the necessity of its end.

I point out this experience from the other side of the healing dyad for a couple of reasons. One is that it is an example of how the healer in me was triggered by my own direct experience of suffering. One not need be a hopelessly addicted person to see, feel and touch this. In fact, I had touched directly upon suffering on thousands of occasions before this one, some in the realm of my addictive life and some not associated with that dilemma. However, for me the suffering ballet played out most dynamically in my active addiction. And when all was said and done, despite my impaired nervous system, I was the one who had the direct experience, the psychic change. At best, my girlfriend was able to facilitate the change through policing and babysitting for hours at a time. The Three Rolling Rock incident finally pushed me toward my sober friend Maggie, instead of away from her, and she became the next agent of change as she gently nudged me into my first AA meeting. And there I found people and a program that had a language and a structure for my continued healing.

How did Maggie and those people at that first meeting arrive there?

Through their own suffering and the admonition of AA that service to others in the same predicament would be the answer to their problem. Essentially, there was enough wisdom to be able to set the intention of staying sober, and then speaking, acting and working in such a way to support that endeavor. These first five factors of the Eight Fold Path – Right Wisdom, Intention, Speech, Action and Livelihood - were thereby manifested. Professional helpers go through much the same vortex. We suffer as all beings born into a body do, and we get moved to compassion first perhaps for others and then ourselves, and we want to help the sufferer. We need somehow to take care of ourselves and find sufficient healing to then have the strength, courage and compassion to help others.

The other reason for the Rolling Rock story is this. Of all the Buddhist wisdom that can guide healers and helpers, the notion that we cannot provide the experience for the client, patient or student is central. We can only point the way. Even when we are in the midst of the most direct or directive of interventions, we are only the facilitator of a process. The great wisdom is that of focusing on myself and my own process, for this is how I will end up of maximum service. Honing in on my own relationship to the Four Noble Truths and the Eight Fold Path can only heighten my skillfulness and my ability to tap into my innate loving kindness, compassion, appreciative joy and equanimity. My own study and contemplation of the timeless wisdom, and my application of it in the world, are how I will become the facilitator, the guide, the spiritual friend. No, not the expert. The friend.

My friend Cindy is an amazing comedian. I have a great number of comedian friends, because I like to laugh, and also because, like the poets and philosophers, comedians often are able to get to the truths of life. Anyway, when Cindy would talk about her therapist, she would always say, "I was talking to my friend that I pay..." She actually captures the essence of helping and healing in this one liner. The wisdom of interconnectedness is the desire to spend one's livelihood in some kind of service to others.

My last thought on the subject for now is this: When I worked as a substance abuse prevention and intervention educator, we told a story to explain the mechanics of informal and formal intervention. We asked participants to imagine a baby born carrying a backpack, an image that brings a smile to most. The baby grows up to be fourteen years old and develops a drinking problem. Then there is that first person ever who says to them, "I'm concerned about you." In most cases the young person tells them to take a hike and mind their own business. But a brick has been placed in the backpack. Then the second person comes and admits to their concern. It may turn the young addict's head for a moment, or he may run away in the other direction. Either way, they are still not ready. Then it's off to college and beyond. And many other bricks go in the backpack. Finally, someone comes to the addict who is now hunched over, still carrying a giant backpack full of bricks. One more person comes and expresses their concern. She puts her brick in the backpack, and finally the young addict puts the backpack down and agrees to get some help. This was not a magic brick. In fact, the last brick would not have worked had not every single one of the other bricks been placed in the backpack.

This is right understanding, the accumulation of the proper wisdom. We can change our karma at any moment. As healers, we can simply and lovingly do our part for each person that comes before us, and no more. Our karma is to heal or help those who come into our path. The karma of those who come for our help is in their hands. Whether it be handing them a brick of intervention, or whether it be the healing touch of our words or actions, we are the stewards of our actions -- and this is whether we believe in a Higher Power or not. Buddha did not ever satisfactorily answer the questions of the afterlife, God or metaphysics -- but he did give an answer for the end of suffering in this lifetime. Our responsibility is to study that wisdom and investigate that understanding in books, with each other, and with our own bodies, thoughts and feelings. And that is how we will connect and heal, human being to human being, moment to moment, day to day.

CHAPTER 6

RIGHT INTENTION

Right Intention

The wisdom of Clinical Dharma is grounded in the Four Noble Truths. Having established the foundation of the first factor of the Eight Fold Path through study, consultation and direct experience, we can now set our intention for how we will move about in the world. As it pertains to our role as helpers, we are in debt to those that have gone before us, all the way back to the Buddha, and even before his time. In order for Buddha to have his own transformative experience, he had to see not only the suffering of sickness, old age and death. He also had to see those who had renounced worldly concerns, the monks and nuns with robes and begging bowls, and varying levels of ascetic practices. He needed to see a model of what might be the alternative to all this suffering. And then he went out and sought after the wisdom of those who had developed a practice and the knowledge that went with it. Siddhartha Gautama was not yet the Buddha when he set this intention. He needed guides; he needed knowledge and to be pointed in the direction of practice.

The Buddha was an extraordinary person inasmuch as he was able to exhaust the wisdom of each of the teachers that he met along the way. As he came to the end of each teacher-student relationship, he could see when the teacher could take him no further. The wisdom he maintained through all these changes was that there was more for him to learn, that he had not yet discovered the end of suffering, and therefore his wisdom journey was not over. Since Buddha taught that we are going to be able to have the same experience that he had, we can let go of the egotistically driven notion that we are exactly like the Buddha and lean into what the Buddha taught, which was that he was a human being who had an experience. We are human beings too; we too can have that experience.

Under those terms, we can look at our lives up until now, our lives in the present, and our lives of intention for the future. We may not always drop teachers when we have exhausted their wisdom and we have surpassed them, but we can see teaching relationships that have had a beginning, a middle and an end. These relationships may have come in the form of books, art, friendship, romance, education, therapy, spiritual practice, or otherwise. Looking back on the past, we can track each of these relationships and see the intention that brought us into them, the intention that fed the work we did together, and the intention (sometimes expressed in seemingly more passive ways) that led us out of that relationship and into our next set of lessons.

The inventory practices of AA, Refuge Recovery and other addiction recovery programs are also found in various therapeutic modalities and are implicit in the simple act of journaling; these all are excellent ways to come upon this information for yourself. Tracking the various relationships and intentions can show us patterns and give us the information and personal wisdom we need to begin setting further intention. My own story of sharing inventory with my sponsor Randy represents a major turning point in my own understanding of this. When I arrived at Randy's apartment to share my inventory, I was expecting a sweaty, tearful eight to twelve-hour experience, including a shamanic burning of the document at the end of the process. Instead, I was greeted by Randy in his workout clothes, stating, "I have to get to the gym in two hours, so let's get started."

Then he commented on the thirty-four-page document in my hands. "What's that? Let me show you my 4th Step." He brought out a one page document in the AA Big Book columns format. I was starting to get worried. Maybe he sensed that, and he asked me to begin reading my work. About ten minutes into the reading, he told me to stop. "Give that to me," he said. He started flipping through it. "This thing is not thirty-four pages long." I was confused. He continued. "This is three pages long, over and over again. You do the same stupid shit to different people three pages at a time."

It makes sense to me with my Brooklyn birth and Randy's Bronx childhood that one of my early spiritual experiences would contain an expletive. My mind was blown. He was right. In that moment I had one of my first adult visceral acknowledgements of thought preceding action, of karma, of intention and its fruits. I could see the cycle in that repetitive thirty-four-page accumulation of unskillful, unwise beliefs and behaviors, leading to setting of intentions that did not have wholesome foundations, leading to actions that were not in the best interest of everyone (sometimes anyone) involved. Of course I was not all "stupid shit" and no wisdom; I was not all bad and no good, but by focusing on these particular negative aspects in this way, I gained that much more insight into my potential ability to set intention from a place of balance.

What does this setting of intention mean for the helper? Many people get into the world of the helping professions from the simplest of intentions -- I want to help. Nothing more than this one seed will sometimes change the trajectory of a person's career and livelihood. Beyond that compassionate and loving desire to help are many nuances of wisdom that develop and nurture that intention.

We can use a couple of the foundational teachings of Buddha as our example of wisdom and its impact on intention. Buddha taught about the Three Poisons -- Greed, Anger and Delusion. These poisons he called the roots of our suffering. What better place to start than at the roots? In addition to those three poisons he named three other roots -- Non-greed, Non-Aversion and Non-delusion. The language and grammar of ancient

India present these as negations of the unwholesome states. Fleshed out into positive qualities, non-greed becomes renunciation, detachment and generosity; non-aversion becomes loving kindness, sympathy/empathy and gentleness; and non-delusion becomes wisdom. Furthermore, Buddha proclaimed ignorance to be the "root of the root."

As the antidote to greed, what wonderful words for helpers -- renunciation, detachment and generosity. Renunciation is that word conjuring up images of shaved heads, begging bowls and robes, but it need not be seen only in that way. The Oxford Dictionary definition of renunciation is the "formal rejection of something, typically a belief, claim, or course of action."
When I set out to help someone, I let go of my belief in the primacy of my needs in the helping dynamic. I release my claim to my ego gratification. And I let go of the greedy sense of I/Me/Mine as a guiding principle in my course of action -- it is transformed into a generosity of spirit regarding the material expressed through time, energy, and service. Detachment allows me to provide loving kindness and attention without getting swept away by the feeling states attached to the experience of the person being helped and generated by my own helping experience. Finally, sometimes generosity seems in such short supply in the 21st century, so that anytime we provide that for a sufferer, we are providing a rare and beautiful visceral resource memory.

As for anger, hatred and aversion, helpers can lean into the feeling/action states of loving kindness, sympathy/empathy and gentleness. All of these reflect the acknowledgement on a deep level of the Noble Truth of suffering. How can we be filled with hatred or aversion for others who simply suffer as we do? We do not come to this conclusion perfectly and forever, but we can cultivate it. Loving kindness is that deep, sincere wish that all beings be freed from suffering. When we are faced with someone in our care, we can allow them (and ourselves) to represent all beings for that moment that we are together, and our loving kindness will by default radiate out in all directions. Many times we will be able to empathize, being able to feel and relate to the experience of the other. Other times we will not relate, and we are only able to sympathize. As long as we are not crossing the boundary of that person's experience with our empathy, or resorting to pity with our sympathy, then we will be able to be of service.

And what of the root of the root? These simple foundational teachings of the Buddha can be enough to guide the intention setting from this point on. Ignorance and delusion come when we complicate things. Life is complicated enough without our using our minds unskillfully to create more layers, more obstacles to our connection to intention. Once I have set the intention to help, to heal, to increase connection and develop a life of service, then I can use the guidance found in the Buddha Dharma to set wise intention moment to moment, hour to hour, day to day, month to month, year to year, and (if you subscribe to it) lifetime to lifetime. Regardless of how far into the future our intention is being set, we can lean back into the wisdom available through study, connection and direct experience, and we can lean forward into the speech and actions that will reflect our intention. And if we are in the helping professions, then that intention will always have the undercurrent and foundation of service.

Thought precedes action, taught the Buddha. Intention begins the process of karma, which simply means action. The next three factors, the ethical factors, are the karmic fruits of our intention. They are the way we move about in the world, and are critical to our understanding and practice of Clinical Dharma.

CHAPTER 7

RIGHT SPEECH

Right Speech

Many years ago I created and ran a Juvenile Diversion program for young people in New York City who had been convicted of hate crimes. Many of the young people I worked with were not entrenched in hate, but rather needed an education about the mechanics of prejudice and discrimination to understand and change their inner and outer interpersonal framework. Some others were truly committed to their beliefs of the inferiority of the other. All of them were brought through a ten-week program where they were introduced to a number of different cultures, as well as lessons in the history and importance of civil rights. Except for the first and last session, I co-facilitated the program with various speakers and educators that included lawyers, civil rights educators, therapists, and other professionals.

One of my partners in this endeavor was a survivor of the Holocaust. He was the oldest of my co-facilitators, and without fail he would be looked upon incredulously by my charges. Then he would go into his story, which took place when he was a little younger than the young people I was working with. As his story progressed, there would almost always be some tears running down cheeks, and questions from the students that indicated that they were trying to rewrite the history to comfort the speaker. And every time, once the story was over, and the emotions in the room were high, he would make his primary point: "The Holocaust did not start with gas chambers," he would say. "It didn't start with guns, or broken glass, or anything like that. The Holocaust started with words." That one word would hang in the air for what seemed like forever. The young faces around us seemed to harden and soften simultaneously. And the two sessions that followed would be more energized. When I think back on those years with that program, I sometimes think that was the moment and the message that created the low recidivism rate amongst my students.

So if words can create the greatest horrors that we have seen, they must also have the power to create the greatest good. Even though it is not necessarily an 8 Step program, it makes sense that Right Speech precedes Right Action. Since thought precedes action, and inner speech is a major element of the thought process and the setting of intention, it is clear that speech has great sway over the resulting actions. Then when we move from our interior experience to the exterior and are engaged in relational mindfulness, our words and our interpretation of the words of the other are going to have a dramatic impact on who does what and how.

Pertaining to Clinical Dharma, words have infinite power to heal or to harm. As human beings, one of the ways we work together on healing projects is through our words, spoken or written. Buddha taught about four forms of speech to stay away from: false speech, slanderous speech, harsh speech, and idle chatter. Just briefly contemplating these four terms, one can start to integrate the wisdom of these admonitions. Then moving toward the positive flip side of these harmful forms of speech, one can see the beauty of speaking the truth, uniting people rather than dividing them, using gentle and soothing words, and saying the right meaningful thing at the right time in the right way.

Although he did not use these words in particular, a central aspect of Buddha's teachings on Right Speech was that one must meet a person where they are. Buddha would speak to each person and each audience in such a way as to help them to end their suffering. This looks different to diverse groups of people. Many years ago, I went to hear the Dalai Lama speak at Central Park in front of an audience of thousands. I was there with my friend who was a Tibetan nun. The next day, she had the opportunity to hear him speak in front of about 100 monastics. She said that the talks were very different. The Dalai Lama's goal was not to impress people, or to speak above their heads or below their level of training. His goal, like the Buddha's, was to teach suffering and the end of suffering. Professional helpers are tasked with the same ethical duty.

My experience in the addiction world frames this well. More than once in my practice I have had a client come in who is a few days sober from meth and heroin. They are in physical discomfort and emotional distress, and they are unsure about whether or not they want to be sober. The next client comes in, and they are seventeen years sober and have been having a high-functioning and happy life, when suddenly traumatic memories from the past resurface, and they are having trouble sleeping. They feel off their game. They are not necessarily feeling near a relapse, but they are aware that if they don't take care of this trauma resurgence, things might lead in that direction. If I were to use the same words, the same content, the same facilitative measures with these two clients, somebody is not going to get what they need, or even may be harmed. If I look at these two clients with a cookie cutter attitude, regardless of which direction I skew with my cookie cutter, I will not be able to help either one of them.

In order to provide the best care, I need to use words that reflect my deepest intention to meet them where they are, not force them to meet me where I am, or where I think they should be. I want to come to them from my truth, and, hopefully, that truth is grounded in loving kindness and compassion. I want to find words that help generate the relational bond between us, but most importantly, provide a context for the internal deepening of the integration experience for the client.

In my work as a Substance Abuse Prevention and Intervention educator, we would teach young people and families about the steps in an informal intervention. The key to the success of any intervention is found in the very first step and it involves words. The person intervening is encouraged to vest the relationship; that is to say, to use caring words that are appropriate to this particular relationship.

There is such power in those words of love and care preceding mentioning any particular concerns, such as the difficult feelings being experienced, or especially the consequences for the addict if they are not able to change. How many times as a clinician have I been told by someone either new or old in my practice that I represent a safe place to say anything, to be themselves, to be honest? It is that first level of safety, that first small space between the disasters and the suffering, that can change the conversational trajectory toward healing.

Sometimes the space is made up of no words at all, at least on my part. Sometimes right speech is abiding by the AlAnon slogan I heard for the first time so many years ago -- "Don't just do something, sit there." I can say the same for the principle of not saying something either. Just sit there. Sometimes that's the hardest thing of all to do. Buddha recommended meditation to develop wisdom and compassion, which then become words and actions. What better way to develop wisdom and compassion regarding the suffering of all beings than to sit still and witness our own inner speech? What am I saying to myself today? Would I allow anyone to talk to my friend or loved one that way? Calming our own minds and reorienting our own inner speech are often the first steps toward having a new way of speaking to others.

As I engage with the world, are my words helpful or harmful? When my words are harmful, they tend to replay in my mind, either because of remorse or continued desire to do more harm. Either way, we are building a fortress of suffering for ourselves. As helping professionals, we need the right words at the right time for the person who is with us at that moment. When I lived at the monastery, the rule of thumb was "no unnecessary speech." Perhaps as I look at my reasons for being in the healing position, I can parse out those that are ego driven, that would love to hear the sound of my own voice bringing wisdom to all. Then my words can be sourced from a place that the Zen teachers call the "beginningless beginning," a place before words and even beyond words. We can find the words that will end suffering, either in the moment or as part of our long-term training of ourselves and others in the dharma of healing. In this way our words will not get in our way or the way of others. Our words will fuel intention on both sides, and the healing of Right Action can begin.

CHAPTER 8

RIGHT ACTION

Right Action

I begin to take action from the moment I wake up in the morning. Often the first action is to open my eyes, and my first choice of the day is whether I will close them again. This can be seen literally and metaphorically. When it is time to wake up, I begin the stream of actions that will often determine the tenor of the remainder of my day. Will I do those non-harmful activities that feed my body and mind so that I might go out and continue to act without harm? Each moment comes complete with a trap door (or two). How do I build my actions, one by one, into a path that can end suffering, first for myself and then for others?

First, I can reach back into the earlier factors for sustenance and guidance. I have built my wisdom to the point where I have a personalized tool kit to work with. I am no longer flying blind, but rather have access to the Three Jewels of Buddha, Dharma and Sangha in order to decide how and when to act. Buddha, or Buddha Nature, allows me to see myself as no different than the historical Buddha, inasmuch as I have the innate potential for enlightenment that the Buddha had. I have been promised that the same direct experience the Buddha had is available to me and to others. The Dharma has been revealed in many forms over the millennia and now is manifesting cross-culturally, and across denominations and belief systems related to the teachings of the Buddha. Our access to the insight brought by the Dharma has been increased and improved, some would say to such a great extent as to be sometimes overwhelming. And the Sangha is growing all the time it seems, the international community, our local communities, and the community of helpers gathered through reading this book or going on retreat.

Now intention can be set from this wisdom of the Three Jewels. That intention was and is invaluable in relation to Right Speech, and it is no different for Action. Going back to when I first open my eyes and engage my other senses first thing in the morning, what is my direct experience of those first moments? How do I choose to interact with them? What is the Dharma of this day? How will I be in my first relational moments of the day if there is a significant other, family, roommate, or pet present? If I live alone, how will I relate to the person in the mirror? Intention is set from this place.

Now comes the time to speak and act. Internal speech probably began from the moment of awakening. Now we open our eyes and begin the actions of the day. Even getting out of bed in the morning is a kind and compassionate action. If you are in the helping professions, especially in more acute types of care, you have probably been in the presence of a sufferer for whom getting out of bed is a challenge. So when we tell that person they have made a great step when they get out of bed after a long period of debilitating depression or other illness, we are not just trying to be an encouraging cheerleader. We know through our own direct experience that taking the action of starting the day is not a given.

In fact, more than one person in more than one spiritual tradition has said so much to me. When I started my journey in EPRA, the Employment Program for Recovering Alcoholics, a non-profit outpatient vocational rehab for addicts, I arrived with some trepidation and doubt. I remember the process of deciding on my clothes, eating breakfast, the long walk to the subway, the crowded subway during rush hour. I remember hating that rush hour subway, something I had avoided for the last number of months as I was on unemployment and using that opportunity to get sober. I remember getting to the building in Midtown, not far from Penn Station, my least favorite part of New York City. I remember entering the nondescript group room, sitting down, and wanting something magical and immediate to happen.

The first "magic" was when two of my friends from AA meetings came in. All three of us brightened at the sight of each other, and our conversation generated a sense of immediate new community. After a few minutes the executive director came in to say a few words to us. He seemed quite happy to see us. "I want to congratulate all of you," he started. "You have officially completed 98 percent of the EPRA program..." He took a breath, scanned the room, and his smile turned serious. "You showed up." All of us in that room had heard this phrase over and over, and here it took on new meaning for me. This was the next level of action, this was the next level of showing up. In order to learn how to show up for life I had to show up to the showing-up workshops and showing-up therapy. It was very much a shift from the immediate gratification template I had been working from for years. Or in Dharma terms, it was a shift from the endless craving, clinging and aversion cycle onto the path of direct experience, curiosity and mindful presence from moment to moment, leading to insight.

How I see this moment of showing up and the acknowledgement provided by the EPRA executive director in the context of Right Action has some layers. First, in the present moment. I see my sitting here writing these words as a direct result of that moment in EPRA long ago. This morning there were several barriers encouraging me to ignore this work. My back is in spasm, my coffee maker is not working properly, and my child looks so darn cute, I just want to wake her up and start hanging out. I have worked my way through these barriers to the laptop and into this conversation with you. This conversation is in turn an amalgam of thousands of conversations and actions over the last twenty-five years. Each one of those actions has been karmic, a dance of cause and effect, each effect having its sway over the next cause.

This directive of taking Right Action becomes much more profound and powerful in the face of the law of karma. According to the Buddha, we own one thing and one thing only -- our karma. We are the owners of our actions. Nothing else belongs to us. In the Clinical Dharma sense, I only have power over my own actions, the decisions that I make and then enact in the course of my work with others. The only sway I have over what happens in the dance outside my realm of influence occurs when my actions have a ripple effect into the karmic realms of others. When I do loving kindness practice, often I start by delivering loving kindness to myself, and then send it out far and wide, often as far as to "all sentient beings in all known and unknown universes." Who is to say if an intergalactic being feels and integrates our silent delivery of loving kindness? However, we can say that I own that choice to send out loving kindness instead of greed, hatred and delusion. So one can say that if we bring it back here to the earthly realm, in our temporal experience, the helper in the presence of the person needing help, our delivery of action steeped in loving kindness may have more tangible and visible results.

Or it may not. That is the tricky part. We own our actions, but we don't own, nor can we predict or force, the results. So when I act, step by step, in the helping fashion that I learned in school or through experience, I can lean deeply into the mystery. That mystery does not have to swallow me up, as in mystery turned to delusion. That mystery can be the spark for infinite curiosity, a deeper investigation, and more actions with a foundation of loving kindness, compassion, appreciative joy and equanimity.

When I was living at the Zen monastery, each morning we would do some chanting. The chant just before the Heart Sutra would announce the unique quality of this day, of this moment. "This Dharma, incomparably profound, and minutely subtle, has not been seen in hundreds of thousands of millions of kalpas." A kalpa is the length of a lot of eons. Needless to say, this moment, if it has ever been perfectly duplicated, that has not been the case for millions and millions of years. There is much wisdom to draw from as I decide what next action to take.

Buddhas, bodhisattvas, arahants, monks, nuns, poor and wealthy, people of many cultures and ethnicities, oppressed and oppressor, those with resources and those in need, all have been faced with decision after decision as to what action to take next. Helpers, in the moment of helping, must use all of this wisdom to fuel our intention. As a wise friend once said, "The power of negative example is just as powerful as the power of positive example. See that guy over there who is fucking things up? Don't be like him." Right Action is born of wisdom, intention, and internal and external speech. Mindfulness applied to each of these results in the possibility of healing and health. Which brings us to the work related aspects of our Actions, the heart of Clinical Dharma -- Right Livelihood.

CHAPTER 9

RIGHT LIVELIHOOD

.

Right Livelihood

I have often joked with participants in Clinical Dharma workshops that we get a free pass on this aspect of the path. These workshops and retreats usually take place at facilities and/or with people where the focus is on identifying suffering and trying to alleviate it. Buddha gave a few instructions about Right Livelihood 2600 years ago, and these included not selling arms or poison, as well as other destructive livelihoods. Those of us in the helping professions or engaging in avocational help are obviously trying to live constructively. So what further can be said about Right Livelihood in this context?

First, we can consider the nature of service. Often service work is defined by providing help without expecting anything in return. In the end, there is a difference between an expectation of a certain result or certain form of payback, as opposed to simply being paid for services rendered. I have often found that people in the helping professions have a hard time charging for what their skills and/or time are worth, and many recipients of this type of help feel like they should not have to pay, or should only pay a limited amount. This can be crippling for both the provider and the person being helped. One can provide help on an ongoing basis pro bono, sliding scale or low fee; that is surely true. I have done so at times in my career, and

I know many who live their lives using this as the guiding rubric. The key is to make sure it is sustainable for both the caregiver and the receiver of the care.

One can use the Three Poisons as part of the guide for our work in this area. Is my service rendered in the spirit of greed, where I am greedy for a certain result, or for adulation, or for a higher fee than the service merits? Is the service in the spirit of ill will or hatred, where my fear and anger are driving my decisions about who to help, and if and how to help them? Is the service in the spirit of delusion and ignorance, where I might be inserting myself into a situation that does not call for my assistance? If I am able to satisfactorily answer these foundational questions, I can look more deeply down into the next layer of the service paradigm.

There are those who frame the service argument a little differently, saying that both the server and the served must find benefit from the interaction if it is to be truly beneficial. What is important here is how we define benefit. The gain for the person receiving the service perhaps is more explicit. I am suffering, I need help, the helper provides that help, and I receive the benefit of that help. The benefit for the service person may be more subtle and implicit, but a benefit nonetheless. In its simplest and maybe even purest sense, the server gets to act on their path factor of Right Livelihood. Just that opportunity indicates that I am on the path to liberation. And this is not a greedy endeavor in that sense. My path to liberation will allow me to participate that much more heartily in the liberation of other beings. Instead of the service draining me and taking from me, it actually propels me toward freedom. When I am in Right Livelihood, much like when I am in Right Speech or Action, I am in the flow of all that feeds and builds, rather than that which would tear at the fabric of my life and that of society.

My further experiences at EPRA after the Day One speech described in the previous chapter gave me additional understanding of Right Livelihood, both as I went through the program and since I have been back in the work world for the past twenty-five years. My own process during the EPRA program involved my wanting them to take me out of the music business and make me into something as concrete and steady as possible, perhaps a plumber. I had felt like making music had become a liability, and that I could not separate my self-destructive behaviors from being a musician. I had a feeling that the lack of structure fed that part of me that made me enter into difficult and draining mind states - states of greed, anger and delusion. In the Judeo-Christian model, idle hands were the devil's playground.

As I progressed through the groups, the therapy, the research and the introspective writing, I started to have more and more clarity about what my next steps might be. I was looking into becoming a freelance writer, although it was lower on my list due to its similarities to music in spare time, self-discipline and potential for bad habits. I was also looking at the profession of teaching, particularly high school English. In considering my various interests over the years and where they might coalesce into a life of creativity and service, I didn't believe that creating art was not an act of service; I just believed that I would not be able to sustain such a life, and that it would keep me from doing the service.

When I was close to finishing the program, I had my closing meeting with the social worker who had been with me since the beginning of my journey. For our final sit-down, we went over all of the work I had done. I remember her having a very kind face, but I did not find it so kind when she delivered her final assessment: "I think you should make music and be a music producer." She was only giving her feedback based on her subjectively objective observation of my process. I was enraged. I wanted to run far away from the world of making music, working freelance, struggling and living without a structured way to make a living. She rated my idea of teaching high school decidedly in second place.

And in the end, I took her suggestion to heart as a backup plan. I turned things on their head in terms of the traditional artist setup. I saw teaching high school English as the dream, with making music as my fall-back option. And as I moved forward with that plan, what was revealed to me was the notion of Right Livelihood as being as true to oneself as one's resources and abilities will allow. I became an English teacher in Crown Heights, Brooklyn. Not long after starting at that job, I found that my need to make music returned and the shortage of time drove me to utilize it wisely. I taught my students during the day, and I wrote songs at night. As I learned how to teach more effectively, I walked in the direction of any resources that might help that journey grow, change and become more of service. I found myself in a graduate program, and then in my second year of teaching I found myself at the heart of learning about conflict resolution, diversity, prejudice and discrimination, and then sharing it with my students. I eventually taught students and teachers all over the country and the world on these topics, all the while writing songs and banging on a drum.

I often credit my first experience doing service in AA as the beginning of my Right Livelihood training. I was nominated several times to help with the coffee at a meeting, and I kept on "humbly declining," to the laughter of the group. I didn't want to admit that I didn't really know how to make a cup of coffee. Finally, a very attractive member of the group said she would make the coffee, and I jumped to my feet to offer my help. When we went to the kitchen to survey the scene, it turned out that neither of us knew how to make coffee, certainly not for 100 people. We got the wisdom and the teaching from the previous maker of the coffee, and we supported each other in the learning. And then over the next six months, I became obsessed with making the best AA coffee in NYC. And I sat by the pot before the meeting so that I could meet people and make sure everything was in good shape.

This all happened before I re-entered the workplace. This spirit of service, of taking risks and of not having to know everything beforehand has guided me to and through my Livelihood up until now. By following the bouncing ball of service-driven Right Livelihood, I have for the most part been able to stay true to myself, and in doing so, to provide truthful and soulful service to others. Always, the goal is to be of help, and not do harm. That goal includes myself. The guiding principle is that all beings be free from fear, healthy, happy and at ease. I am included in all those beings. And then I can engage in my Right Livelihood actions free from fear, healthily, happily and with a sense of ease. With this in mind, in order to deepen the experience of the three ethical factors of Speech, Action and Livelihood, I move into the Mindfulness factors, first that of Effort.

CHAPTER 10

RIGHT EFFORT

Right Effort

My introduction to Dharma practice came at a Zen Buddhist monastery in upstate New York. I was on a retreat designed for working on the AA steps and program. The meditation aspect was low key and kept within the retreat group, which was meeting in a house separate from the main monastery building. When offered the chance to take a meditation lesson from a monastic, there was a decision to make. I could stay in the comfort of the known. I could stay in the same environment with the same people. This safety was not problematic; however, in some ways it spoke to either my unwillingness or inability to move out of a certain zone and dedicate a different type of effort toward my well being. Again, this was not about pathology. It was about effort and direction.

I have a visceral memory of walking out of the retreat house into the brilliant summer sunshine. I remember walking with those of my retreat group who had also agreed to take the meditation lesson. I remember sitting on a round cushion that was placed on top of a larger square cushion. I recall it not being uncomfortable at first, until the first twinge of tightness led to my moving a bit. And then I remember receiving the very simple and wryly delivered instructions: "Sit down. Shut up. Don't move." And then the bell rang.

I have been making an effort to build and maintain mindfulness and concentration ever since. As they say, you cannot unring a bell, and that bell launched me into a new world of the mind and body. That initial effort to walk from one house to another began a life-long journey. And that path has been walked through my dedicated effort ever since. Sometimes I am full of energy. Other times I am without a clue as to how I made it from Point A to Point B. The common thread between those different moments, hours and days has been the effort made to at least get to the place where effort could be made.

In the Clinical Dharma sense, I need to know a proper direction for my healing energy as well as the indicated level of strength. When I teach meditation in therapeutic settings, I often will give a guarantee to the participants. I tell them if you do this practice for five minutes a day for two weeks, you will see at least a small decrease in whatever your current symptoms are, anxiety, for instance. You will also see at least a small increase in your level of focus. This guarantee is built out of years of experience both sitting and teaching. And it also reflects further the snowball nature of much of the practice. I put in the effort to do five minutes a day. Through that simple practice I develop at least the first level of mindfulness: the mindfulness of how mindful I fail to be in many moments. I then apply and deepen my concentration in order to find some peace between the thought raindrops. And this growing mindfulness and concentration emboldens me to further my efforts on my own behalf.

One of the first rounds of effort I need to make is knowing when to use the accelerator and when to hit the brakes. I also need to know how to sometimes feather the pedal, and how to use the brakes in such a way that I do not screech to a halt. This of course comes with practice and with time. However, beginning as soon as possible to make an effort to find a balanced way to apply effort can be the make-or-break crossroads for anyone on this path of providing healing. If I am driving at a hundred miles an hour with an intention to get where I am going without regard for the journey, the scenery, the nuances and the possible obstacles, I can find myself injured and unable to continue with my work. If I hit the brakes hard at every stop light, I will dissolve the brakes to dust and will not have the ability to stop and consider next moves in any situation. Burnout can have a lot of ramifications, not least of which is our own deterioration and the simultaneous decline of those we are trying to help. We can cause this burnout on either side of the equation, acceleration or braking, or both. We want to accelerate to excel, and brake instead of break.

The Buddhist teaching on effort focuses on four types of effort, all of which are pertinent for the healer. The first is the effort to avoid. This can be illustrated most clearly in the treatment of addiction. The first thing that the addict needs to do is to avoid acting out on the addiction. Until the acting out itself stops, it is very hard to implement new thoughts and behaviors. And in that regard, we know from Right Intention preceding the ethical factors of Speech, Action and Livelihood that thought precedes action. So our effort goes toward avoiding those thoughts that will lead to those actions that will continue the addiction. This is not a simple act of escape. It can be from time to time, but that by itself is not sustainable. We can see that in the very nature of addiction, which is a method of escape that may work for a time but is very limited in the shelf life of its efficacy. The effort to avoid is made through practicing mindfulness and concentration in such a way that one's relationship with one's thoughts changes. Once that relationship has changed to one of more objective awareness, it becomes much easier to make choices about which thoughts and actions to avoid, and which to walk toward and cultivate.

Then comes the effort to eliminate those unskillful qualities that have already arisen. Not all of our efforts at restraint and healthy avoidance will be successful. In addiction recovery terms, this can be related to my approach to relapse with a client. Most relapses I have borne witness to are accompanied by shame and a sense of despair. There is not an increased desire to make an effort to avoid further relapse, but rather a resignation to the status quo, the client's perceived ultimate truth that they cannot get better. When I sit with someone who has recently relapsed, the first job is shame reduction and the avoidance of continued unskillful action. We try to see the relapse in the context of the story of recovery, rather than as a singular statement on the person's existence. In this way, we can chart a course of day-to-day, moment-to-moment abandonment of the unskillful qualities that lead to their suffering. In this way we practice the abandonment of unskillful qualities that have arisen.

The third and fourth efforts of Buddha's list cover those qualities that will lead to a skillful life. This implies that even though there are qualities of the Buddhist path that arise naturally from a small and simple degree of practice, we must make an effort to cultivate these skillful means as well. Buddha gave us more than a sense that the catapult for all of these skillful traits is mindfulness and concentration. Through effort devoted to these practices come all good things. Loving kindness, compassion, appreciative joy and equanimity blossom from these practices. Mindfulness and concentration behave as a vortex through which we land in states of energy, tranquility, even rapture. And through these states, we find ourselves deepening our peaceful presence, wishing less harm and desiring more healing for ourselves and others. The loving kindness and compassion born of mindfulness and concentration is far more powerful than love and compassion which has not allowed itself to integrate into the bones and marrow through dedicated practice. Through this practice we find we can cultivate our speech, actions and livelihood in a whole new way. Through our efforts we help these states to arise in us. There is nothing forced. We create an entire world of healing simply through the effort of our attention.

Once these states have arisen, we now need to maintain them. That is the fourth and perhaps most crucial effort. Without this type of effort, we will inevitably fall back into unskillful ways. I have learned this from experience. My own behavioral relapses, where I overwork, where I overeat, where I fall into angst, all of these come from a lack of maintenance of my gains made through practice. I am reminded of my koan practice at the Zen monastery (koans are Zen training tools - stories or sayings that challenge the rational mind and help to deepen insight). Whenever I would get to the end of a koan and even answer it, apparently to my teacher's satisfaction, there would still be tester koans to follow to make sure everything was in place. And in the end, I was instructed that each koan was a lifetime practice, not a mathematical problem to solve. We are not in a race to a finish. We are in a steady gait, walking a path, working together to heal ourselves and others. If we have a wise and discerning eye toward that kind of horizon, we can maintain those qualities that are skillful. We can continually come back to our base. Our base is mindfulness, a very powerful starting point for any attempt at healing words or actions. It is the basis of our loving kindness, compassion, appreciative joy and equanimity. From that balanced place we investigate this matter of mindfulness more deeply.

CHAPTER 11

RIGHT MINDFULNESS

Right Mindfulness

What Buddha created in his psychological and spiritual path that sets it apart from what came prior is this element of mindfulness. Many psychologies and spiritual practices that Buddha found during his own search were in some ways designed to provide temporary escape through bliss, or through simply turning away from the pain of life. What Buddha found through his own investigation of the mind and body was that in order to end suffering one needed to turn toward the pain, toward the suffering. Rather than disconnecting from painful states and difficulties, one had to cultivate a mindfulness of all of it, every aspect of life. In his day and to this day, it can seem counterintuitive, fighting against our instincts for self preservation, the instinct to run from pain and lean into pleasurable states. His own mindful consideration of these states, however, found them all to be impermanent, impersonal and unsatisfactory in the end.

The Buddha provided many explicit teachings on mindfulness, most of which are pertinent in our consideration of Clinical Dharma, the healing of the healer, and the healing that then radiates outward. A primary teaching is the Four Foundations of Mindfulness, or the Satipatthana Sutta. Seen from the Clinical Dharma perspective, this teaching gives us an anchor for our practice and a marker for our progress. The first foundation is that of mindfulness of the body. When we consider our helping careers, are we not at the very base of it human beings attempting to help other human beings (or other sentient beings)?

I am reminded of a teaching I received while living at the monastery. I was in the midst of an average middle of the day zazen sitting, when all of a sudden I had this very extraordinary yet very ordinary sense of myself and my place in the world. I cycled quickly through tranquility, bliss, equanimity, and pure excitement. I remember cycling more than once through these states. When the time for the opportunity to meet with the teacher came, I bolted off my cushion to line up for interviews. My turn came; I rang the bell twice to announce my impending arrival. I went into the interview room in the usual way, and on this particular journey at no time did I lay my eyes on the teacher. Then as I came out of my last prostration and onto my knees, I alerted a curious Roshi as to my experience.

"Roshi!" I shouted. "I just realized that I am a human being -- sitting on the ground!" He smiled. He turned his gaze away, and then back toward me. "How old are you?" he asked plainly, almost seeming like he was having a different conversation. "Thirty-six," I replied. He paused. He smiled. He nodded. He scratched his chin, and with a look of being mildly impressed he said, "Not bad!" And he rang the bell to announce the end of the interview.

I was flooded with all kinds of conflicting emotions as I went back to sit more zazen. My spiritual egotist wanted to be told he was fully enlightened. My spiritually greedy person wanted to cycle some more through those very pleasant states. The fearful low self-esteem aspect of myself went into a spin as to whether or not my breakthrough was acknowledged or even worth acknowledging. And my human being sitting on the ground started to realize it was nearly lunchtime and became hungry. That hunger threw me back into a state of mindfulness, the recognition once again that I was a human being, sitting on the ground, noticing the smells coming from the kitchen and the growling in my stomach.

My ego, my low self-esteem, all of those are thought forms generated by my greed, anger and delusion. Mindfulness allows me to greet and then investigate all of these states instead of rejecting them, fighting them, or ignoring them. Mindfulness allows me to see the simplicity of the experience of my breathing body, moment to moment, as opposed to being driven and thrown around by my thoughts and feelings. As I deepen my experience of mindfulness of the body through breath meditation, body scans, and the investigation of the sense doors and the material entering those doors, my ability to maintain presence in this moment increases. As my ability to stay right here, right now expands, I become more open to my experience in the moment. And then -- I am a human being sitting on the ground.

What better tool can there be for helping others? I know from years in the therapy room that my single greatest gift I give is the gift of my presence. It is most obvious when I sit with someone whose life has been filled with pain and neglect, and I notice there is something or someone in the room besides the two of us. Sometimes the client will notice it before I do. When the feeling of being seen and heard is rare in someone's life, that one moment of seeing and hearing can seem to grow a moment into a thousand lifetimes. It may not be a cure for the rest of the person's life, but it is the portal through which even greater healing can be accessed. That presence becomes the source of mindfulness sufficient to set a new course, the Eight Fold Path and all that it offers the sufferer.

How can we offer mindfulness and concentration as a solution unless we find a way to a practice ourselves? In the addiction world, there are many who profess the attitude that only an addict can help another addict. For many years, I held this belief, until I received amazing spiritual and psychological sustenance from helpers who did not have the same substance and behavioral addictions I had. What they did have was mindfulness that had created for them a very deep understanding of the human experience, which includes craving, aversion, clinging and attachment, and all the attendant suffering that goes along with those states. Perhaps this is the prerequisite for the healing professions, above and beyond that of going through the same exact suffering.

Just recently I was running a mindfulness group at an outpatient rehab. On this day it was a small group, and three of the participants had been working with me for awhile. They had heard a number of my stories related to my long-term recovery, how mindfulness entered my life, my stay at the monastery, and the myriad ways mindfulness practice influences and drives my thoughts and actions. Before going into my agenda for the day, they took the opportunity to ask me some clarifying questions about all this, and their questions indicated that they were truly invested in seeing how mindfulness practice could be relevant in their own lives in recovery. There seemed to be a deeper than usual connection between us all in the room, and all the participants relayed that sentiment at the end of the Q and A. Then we talked about how Right Intention could be seen as maintaining the Right Attitude toward life and toward ourselves, a teaching I had listened to earlier that morning on Gil Fronsdal's podcast. Lastly, we practiced together, a guided loving kindness practice, with a special accent on sending the loving kindness toward ourselves. They thanked me for the group, some with bowing, some with high fives.

As I gathered my thoughts in the room afterwards, I felt a deeper understanding of how mindfulness training works in the clinical setting. One element I felt particularly strongly was the sense of "if he can do it, I can do it." We were not connecting so much at the level of fellow sufferers, but rather in the realm of being fellow mindfulness practitioners. Anyone trained by me knows that I take great pains to normalize that which is normal -- the endless flow of thoughts coming from our brains. And from that normalization comes the democracy of our suffering and the potential for the end of our suffering. "Even those who have practiced for just one sitting," wrote Hakuin in the Song of Zazen, "will be blessed most infinitely."

Each five-minute sitting is a timeless foray into the realm of the beginningless beginning, the groundless ground. Whether it is the first time and the mind never stops, or it is twenty-five years into practice and a deep samadhi is deepened, we are all practicing mindfulness. As helpers, it is not only our helping ourselves through mindfulness to a greater understanding and deeper wisdom that takes our ability to heal to another level. It is our willingness to follow through in our practice in order to be a living, breathing model of the mindful life. If I am willing to walk the Eight Fold Path, my client may be more willing to do the same.

For years I have told my students and clients that five minutes a day is better than thirty minutes on Saturday and no sitting the rest of the week. If that is true for them, it must be true for me. So I go to the teachings of the Buddha and to the teachers who followed over the last 2600 years for guidance, and I sit down, I shut up, and I don't move. I walk the path. And as my teacher said to me many years ago, through my walking that path along with sangha members, clients, students, spiritual friends -- we can all

one day walk shoulder to shoulder.

CHAPTER 12

RIGHT CONCENTRATION

Right Concentration

We live in an ADD world. The words Attention Deficit Disorder all put together in one phrase is a modern invention. And in many ways, the difficulty we classify as ADD is also a modern invention. When Buddha taught his disciples about concentration, there were far fewer distractions in life than there are now. However, the fact that Buddha looked into his mind and found the same foundations of greed, anger and delusion 2600 years ago that we still see today shows us that the mind itself is an infinitely powerful potential source of difficulty and suffering without any external assistance. When it comes to developing concentration, we are faced with an intense array of modern distractions, concerns and mental playgrounds. These are found both internally and externally. My computer, my phone, all the content that lives in cyberspace and can be accessed through devices, traffic, the 24-hour news cycle, global connectedness, texting substituting for live conversation, falsely intimate anonymous comment sections on websites -- the list goes on and on. How could anyone get concentrated in a world such as this? This is perhaps one of the most common questions that our people bring to us in our helping practices, even though it is often unspoken.

The answer that the Buddha found and thus a defining aspect of Clinical

Dharma is that one can become more concentrated anywhere, anytime. Of course going on retreat and minimizing distractions, having people take care of your food and shelter needs so that you might deepen your practice, these all improve the prognosis for becoming more concentrated. But Buddha said we become able to maintain mindfulness in all postures, whether we are sitting, walking, lying down or standing. He also suggested that we could use simple instructions to find our concentration on a regular basis, again in all these postures. My friend and colleague Nancy O'Hara wrote a book in 1995 called Find A Quiet Corner, containing her assessment and advice on developing a concentration and mindfulness practice in the midst of a busy urban life. Just the title implies that one needs simply to seek the quiet corner, and then utilize it. We as helpers can be the pioneers by finding those quiet corners for ourselves. When it comes to right concentration in this framework, we must be willing to discover and then dive into these opportunities for development of concentration. We can look at it from the Rogerian perspective of developing a more nuanced ability to enter the world of the person we are helping, and we can also see it from the Buddhist perspective of developing a foundation of concentration and mindfulness in order to end or at least transform our own suffering and the suffering of others.

The teaching of the Four Foundations of Mindfulness provides a pathway for the healer. The four foundations of mindfulness could also be called the

Four Main Objects of Meditation. When we are practicing Mindfulness of the Body, we are utilizing the breath, the body sensations, and the insight into the impermanent, unsatisfactory and impersonal nature of the body to develop our concentration. When we practice with Mindfulness of Feeling Tone, we are both delving into and simplifying the construct of our internal analysis of our moment-to-moment experience. Instead of lengthy internal narratives about our experience, born of the monkey mind that chases thoughts with other thoughts, we stop for a moment at each sensation, thought, pain, pleasure -- and subject it to the rating scale of pleasant, unpleasant or neutral. This both brings us closer to the direct experience of the painful, pleasurable or neutral moment, and also slows down our mental processes and laser focuses them on what is contained in the moment at hand.

When we move on to Mindfulness of Mind, we are now applying mindfulness to what we previously perceived as either an enemy or an insurmountable peak. Once our concentration and mindfulness powers are more developed and grounded, we are able to remain concentrated on and mindful of the greater field of our thoughts without getting caught up in them. Finally, when we go to Mindfulness of Dharmas, we enter the realm of those truths that we have been striving to understand, and now can place our concentration and mindfulness upon them to take us to a new realm of greater wisdom, leading to the opportunity for even deeper practice. From there we find all the noted states of our progress toward equanimity -- the rapture, the happiness -- the equanimity that leads to even greater concentration... and from here we can find ourselves in the neighborhood of enlightenment.

If it sounds pie in the sky or just not what you are interested in, or perhaps not what you believe in, let's take a step back. Buddha's goal was to understand suffering, and through that understanding and following a path to liberation, to end suffering. Any helper's credo can be boiled down to this essence. So whether there is a major metaphysical component to your orientation as it relates to helping, or if there is a deeply humanistic, atheistic foundation, or any of the other orientations on the continuum -- it is hard to argue with the call to understand suffering and to desire and forge a path toward the end of suffering, or at least its transformation.

So Buddha's initial encouragement toward a concentration practice is this: to explore objects of investigation, those objects we can find right here in our own bodies and minds, so that we might change our relationship to them. His purpose of then having concentration at the tail end of the Eight Fold Path has two major purposeful prongs to it. One is that concentration will bring us back around to the other factors of the path with a quieter mind, and that type of mind will be more able to follow the path. It also indicates that although concentration practice itself is not the end goal of

Buddhist mindfulness, it deepens the other factors of the path and also becomes a core component of that which we label the enlightenment experience.

Over the years, my own concentration practice has shown me the nature of that experience, simply through fairly consistent, dedicated practice. I first saw how scattered my mind was in its untended state. I would sit down, a bell would ring, and the monkey in my mind started swinging from the trees. Then, through consistently bringing the attention back to the breath, I became aware of the monkey. Soon through more concentration I was able to have agency over the monkey. From there, I could move on to a deepening of the focus on the object of meditation. The monkey would sometimes be going from branch to branch in the background, occasionally in the foreground, but my power of concentration was becoming fine tuned in such a way that I could dive within, not just for the sake of diving in, but rather to allow concentration to inform and then become mindfulness.

For a long time, I simply noticed that my focus was greater, my mind and heart were calmer, and my ability to stay clear of past tripping or future tripping was growing. Just these benefits changed the way I did everything. Everything became an object of meditation, a potential mindfulness and concentration practice. And as I wove the practice into my life, the ethical factors of the path took on a new shape as well. Living within the boundaries of those factors no longer was tinged with obligation, but rather was almost fully a desired way of being. As my life became more centered and helpful to others, my mind quieted even more, leaving more room for my mindfulness and concentration.

As I explored other objects of meditation beside the breath, even more growth and change became available. As I could get a real sense of impermanence through concentration, I was able to more naturally let go of all things, seeing their impermanence. As I contemplated the unsatisfactoriness of life in its usual presentation, I grew in great compassion for myself and others, all of us struggling with these many faces of suffering, from the mild to the severe. As I started to let go of an idea of self, my ego deflated just enough to intermingle with the impermanence and deep insight into suffering, which provides me with the humility to forge ahead with my helping career.

All of these are the gifts of concentration, and concentration is the gift of a live lived on the path. We often speak of the Dharma as a wheel, and this portal of concentration leads to reentry into more concentration; this seems to propel us through that wheel. As I allow myself to focus, to concentrate, to go against the stream of the normal buzz of life, I allow myself access to the Dharma. And this is the foundation and the impetus for the Clinical Dharma path. I develop my own practice, for that is the only way I will truly be of help to the sufferer. They do not need to hear what I read in a book. They need to be guided to as direct an experience as possible of this life with all its pain and triumph by someone who has been willing to go there. And then, as my teacher said, we walk shoulder to shoulder, concentrated and mindful. This is the path of the healer and the helper. The selfless expression of the direct experience of the mindfulness described by Buddha 2600 years ago.

CHAPTER 13

THE PATH FORWARD

The Path Forward

Having considered Four Noble Truths and the Eight Fold Path from the perspective of the helper, where does the path lead now? I wrote this book because I have been the witness to so much suffering, including my own. Much of my own suffering came in my early years, especially once I was caught in the web of addiction. When I sobered up at the age of twenty-six, I responded very strongly to the call to service that the 12 Steps proposed. My introduction to Buddhist teachings, precepts and ethics followed shortly thereafter. Between the two, I found myself with a very deeply ingrained and then emerging and evolving desire to be helpful. It began avocationally at AA meetings and in between meetings, and then manifested itself during my vocational rehab experience, leading into my first service-related job as a high school teacher. It is the suffering that has been a part of this journey as a helper and healer until this day that has moved me to create Clinical Dharma as a class series and to write this book as a meditative guide, either in conjunction with the classes or on its own.

The other impetus for this book has to do with my understanding of Buddhism and mindfulness as it has progressed in the late 20th and early 21st centuries. This has included its introduction and spreading to the West, the growth of meditative practices described by the Buddha outside the monastic world, and the introduction of mindfulness into the realm of Western psychology. All of these developments have their positive ramifications and also their challenges. I have been both a participant and a passive observer of these events, and all of them have had a direct effect on my life as an educator and therapist, husband and father, and human being walking the earth.

The arrival of the Dharma in the West obviously had an impact on me, since if this had not occurred I would not be practicing, nor would I have a sangha such as I do. I have directly experienced the power of meditating and practicing as part of a group. Time after time in meditation classes, both as a teacher and as a participant, I hear the complaint of how difficult it is to meditate at home without a sangha. I can attest to that myself, even after years of meditating. Of course there is the long tradition of hermit monks and nuns, and people living and practicing in caves or moving from mountain top to valley to mountain top. However, if we are going to support the practice of lay people in the 21st century, what does that look like?

That is one of the purposes of this small book. Sangha takes many forms. It can be that of geography: I practice with others who live nearby. It can be that of the teachings of a particular teacher or community over podcast or video, much like I have seen with a number of my teachers. It can also be one on one teaching delivered by someone locally or over Skype. There is also the sangha of affinity and social justice action groups, such as the POC/Ally Group at Against the Stream and similar groups within other sanghas. Clinical Dharma is created in response to what I saw as the need for a sangha of helping and healing practitioners. There are two major aspects of this perceived need. One is to provide a portal into Buddhist practice for the myriad of healers who may have been introduced to them but have not found a full expression of the practice. The other is to support the work of the growing number of clinicians and helpers either exploring the Buddhist path or fully embedded there. I felt this need myself more than twenty-five years ago when I first started sponsoring people in AA, and that need has never left me. My hope is that in some small way, the Clinical Dharma community can provide a particular understanding of the 4 Noble Truths, a greater embodiment of the 8 factors of the 8 Fold Path in the helping and healing work of those that seek the path, and a 21st century pathway to reduced burnout within the healing professions, and a higher quality of internal and external life for the healer and the healed.

Perhaps a story or two from my own current and future path can further clarify the path forward. Only a couple of years ago I was contemplating leaving the world of addiction treatment. I had my own cases of burnout since entering the field in 2002, upon my arrival in Los Angeles. I also had been witness to, and directly affected by, the seeming torrent of ethical breaches occurring in the field. Granted, anywhere I have gone during my career I had found the good eggs and the bad ones. I remember back in my high school teaching days when during a parent teacher night a family came to me in tears after a science teacher had pretty much stomped on my student's dreams of becoming a doctor someday. The message delivered to her had been inappropriate as well as incorrect.

In any case, I found myself at a crossroads (again) having been disappointed in attempts to change the way addiction treatment was delivered, even finding myself abused by business associates with questionable ethical motives. At this particular crossroads (which included turning fifty), I returned to what I had always experienced as a solution, which was to pay attention to the words on the many coins I received during my AA sobriety: "To Thine Own Self Be True." That is when I recommitted firmly to the two therapeutic paths I had seen to be effective healers, Buddha Dharma and Eye Movement Desensitization Reprocessing (EMDR) therapy. Having gone to interfaith ministry school, I was aware of and still utilize many other spiritual paths in my work. Having been around the trauma therapy world for many years, I was introduced to and have incorporated many other therapeutic models into my work as a clinician. However, the psychology and spiritual path described and practiced by the Buddha and subsequent teachers and students, and EMDR therapy as designed by Dr. Francine Shapiro and further researched and modified by those that followed her, these were the defining ingredients of what I deemed true for myself as a healer.

So, my initial stalled attempts to help Noah Levine develop Refuge Recovery Centers were reinvigorated, and that journey began. I connected more directly with my colleague and friend Dr. Jamie Marich, who shared my desire to connect mindfulness and EMDR, and who had developed an EMDR International Association (EMDRIA) Approved Basic Training program in EMDR therapy. She helped me finish my Approved Consultant training, and I joined the faculty of her Institute for Creative Mindfulness. Shortly after the establishment of the rehab center, I came to Noah and suggested that we try using EMDR therapy as a primary modality, and that we also see if my proposed use of the 8-phase protocol of EMDR as an agency template would also be supported. That meeting lasted about ten minutes, with Noah trusting my instincts and supporting my efforts.

The path forward from that meeting has been anything but easy, with further training for myself, followed by the training of clinicians within Refuge and then beginning my public-facing trainings in EMDR. All the while, Clinical Dharma was coming together as another aspect of my truth. I have found myself at this time doing only what I believe in, utilizing methods and theoretical orientations that I believe in and working on providing the type of care that I believe in. This is not to say that this has never been the case, of course. It is only to say that I started from the Shakespearean admonition, which led me squarely back to the middle of the truths and path of the Buddha.

Perhaps this is the paradoxical (at least in the Buddhist sense) core of Clinical Dharma. Buddha taught us to look deeply into impermanence, into the unsatisfactory nature of things, and into the selfless nature of our karmic existence. Impermanence can be investigated quite intensely in the world of the healer. Yoga poses lead to the next pose. The nurse witnesses the healing of an ailment, or the decay toward death. The psychotherapist witnesses the flow of one thought form to another, the dance of schemas across the background of the client's mind. The pastoral counselor guides the seeker through the path of life after life.

Unsatisfactoriness or suffering is also a fairly easy object of investigation for the helper. If anything, it can be taken for granted since it is both the creator of our intention to help, and it is the speech, action and livelihood that follows. The helper, it seems, can never escape from this inquiry. The key is not getting sucked into the suffering, not going into the monkey mind flow of the unsatisfactoriness, but rather being able to establish mindfulness of suffering as a base of operations.

The seeming paradox comes from Buddha's counsel to consider deeply the nature of not-self or no-self. Here is where 21st century psychologists may still take issue with the Buddha. There is no need to take issue though. In our modern world with our more complicated and layered bevy of problems, perhaps there needs to be an initial building or rebuilding of the structure of the self in order to investigate selflessness. My therapist Simon from New York often stated that therapy was an ongoing act of reparenting. So if we can reparent ourselves and heal attachment wounds, that is where the work of deconstructing the self can begin. Again, a seeming paradox, but only another way of framing the ongoing study of our body, feeling states, our minds and the myriad dharmas.

I often tell the story of the day that the deer looked right through me. It was after a retreat while I was living at the monastery. It was after lunch during the brief free time before the afternoon work period. I would often go out for a walk in the woods during this time. It was a particularly beautiful day -- blue skies with some puffy clouds, a breeze, the crispness of autumn in the air. I bounded out the monastery door with a spring in my step, having been energized by the retreat, and also because I adored taking these walks. I took a few steps and then glanced to my left and was transfixed. I say transfixed even though I believe this all happened in a heartbeat. I was eyeball to eyeball with a young deer. And I had the experience of being seen and being looked right through simultaneously. On the more worldly plane, the deer seemed to be saying, "I don't need a girlfriend and a record deal to be okay. And it's not just because I don't have a prefrontal cortex either. How about you?" On a more metaphysical plane, his lack of self looked deeply into my own lack of a self that I could land on and I returned the gaze of selflessness, having had my sense of a self blown apart by the deer.

What followed was about two hours of uninterrupted laughter. That's all I remember. I couldn't stop laughing. It was my love of comedy, it was unbridled joy, it was freedom. Freedom from self apparently was the most hilarious and joyful possibility in the world. I don't necessarily consciously bring myself back to that moment again and again in my life as a helper, but between the conscious and unconscious remembrance, I found a renewable source of the grounding in the groundlessness that Pema Chodron often describes.

There is no magic formula to arrive at this. There is only practice. The path forward is the development of one's own mindfulness practice. The more that practice can be rooted in the 4 Noble Truths and the 8 Fold Path, the better, regardless of any other spiritual or religious affiliation or practice. Mindfulness grounded in the ethical factors seems crucial in considering the life of the helper. I believe it is crucial, period. Looking at the path through the lens of Clinical Dharma can be a support to your practice, an energizer of your practice and a frame for your practice.

My hope is the same one that I share at the end of most of my classes and groups of all kinds, that one or two aspects of this book have helped you in any way. My hope is that your life as a helper and healer is made more sustainable. My hope is that your human life can touch others and be healed in return. May all beings be free from fear. May all beings be healthy. May all beings be happy. May all beings be at ease. I look forward to continuing on the path with you.

GLOSSARY

Alcoholics Anonymous (AA) - The 12 step program born in 1935 through a conversation between Bill Wilson and Dr. Bob Smith in Akron, Ohio. The program was put into book form in 1939. Millions of people have been through the program since, and dozens of other programs have come from it.

Arahant - A person who has advanced through practice to enlightenment, or Nirvana.

Bodhisattva - A person who delays entering Nirvana in order to save more beings.

Buddhism - A variety of denominations, philosophies and spiritual practices derived from the teaching of the historical Buddha 2600 years ago. It is one of the world's major religions.

Dharma - With a capital D it refers to the wisdom espoused by the Buddha and his later adherents. With a small d it refers to things, all manifest things and ideas.

Dukkha - Suffering, or unsatisfactoriness.

Eight Fold Path - The prescription provided by the Buddha as his fourth noble truth.

Five Hindrances - These are the hindrances to keeping our practice: Sense Pleasures, Ill will, sloth/torpor/sleepiness, restlessness/worry, and doubt.

Four Foundations of Mindfulness - A primary teaching of the Buddha where he suggests we investigate through mindfulness the elements of Body, Feeling Tone, Mind and Dharmas.

Four Noble Truths - The Basic Teaching of the Buddha on suffering and the end of suffering.

Karma - Cause and effect, the sum total of our actions.

Koan - A spiritual device in Zen Buddhism. A story or saying designed to help the student break through to awakening.

Nirvana - The state in which there is neither suffering, desire, nor sense of self. One is released from the effects of karma and the cycle of death and rebirth.

Not-self (or no-self) - The teaching that states that due to impermanence and other factors, there is no concrete self to land on when considering the self. Deep seeing into this helps bring on awakening.

Roshi - Title for Zen Master.

Sangha - Community, in particular, a community of practitioners of mindfulness.

Satipatthana Sutta - The teaching on the Four Foundations of Mindfulness.

Three Marks of Existence — Impermanence, Unsatisfactoriness, and the Impersonal nature of existence.

The Three Poisons - Greed, Ill-Will and Delusion.

12 steps - The program laid out by Alcoholics Anonymous based on love and service.

Zazen - Literally, "sitting Zen."

Zen - A form of Buddhism that developed when it traveled from India to China and then Japan and other countries in Asia. It picked up spiritual and cultural elements from those cultures.

.

Printed in Poland
by Amazon Fulfillment
Poland Sp. z o.o., Wrocław